Psychologists and Their Theories for Students

Product Manager
Meggin Condino **Project Editor**
Kristine Krapp **Editorial**
Mark Springer

Indexing Services
Katherine Jensen **Rights and Aquisitions**
Margaret Abendroth, Ann Taylor **Imaging and Multimedia**
Robyn Young, Lezlie Light, Dan Newell **Product Design**
Pamela A. Galbreath **Manufacturing**
Evi Seoud, Lori Kessler © 2005, 2015 Gale, a part of Cengage Learning Inc.

For more information, contact
Gale, an imprint of Cengage Learning
27500 Drake Rd.
Farmington Hills, MI 48331-3535

Or you can visit our Internet site at
http://www.gale.com

ALL RIGHTS RESERVED

LIBRARY OF CONGRESS CATALOGING-IN-PUBLICATION DATA

Psychologists and their theories for students / Kristine Krapp, editor.

   p. cm.

      Includes bibliographical references and index.
      ISBN 0-7876-6543-6 (set : hardcover : alk. paper) —
      ISBN 0-7876-6544-4 (v. 1) —
      ISBN 0-7876-6545-2 (v. 2)
      1. Psychologists. 2. Psychology.
      I. Krapp, Kristine M.

BF109.A1P72 2004

150'.92'2—dc22   2004011589

Printed in the United States of America 10 9 8 7 6 5
4 3 2 1

Carl Ransom Rogers

1902–1987

AMERICAN PSYCHOLOGIST, PROFESSOR

COLUMBIA UNIVERSITY, Ph.D., 1931

BRIEF OVERVIEW

Experience is, for me, the highest authority. The touchstone of validity is my own experience. No other person's ideas, and none of my own ideas, are as authoritative as my experience.... Neither the Bible nor the prophets—neither Freud nor research—neither the revelations of

God nor man—can take precedence over
my own direct experience.

These words, from Carl Rogers's classic book
On Becoming a Person, probably best describe
Rogers's contributions to the study of psychology.
Neither the Bible, from which his mother had taught
him, nor the Freudian tenets so popular among his
colleagues could make Rogers conform to the
prevalent views of his time. He stubbornly refused
to follow the perceptions of others. Rogers relied
solely on his own personal experience rather than
on dogma.

Carl Rogers practiced psychotherapy his way
for over 50 years. He never earned the adoration of
those considered the intelligentsia, either in the
United States or the rest of the world, as did
Sigmund Freud and other luminaries of the
twentieth-century mental health movement. Yet in
the introduction to *The Carl Rogers Reader,* a
biography that was published posthumously in
1989, authors Howard Kirschenbaum and Valerie
Henderson note that Rogers was "the most
influential psychotherapist in American history."
Five years before Rogers's death, a 1982 study
published in the journal *American Psychologist*
ranked the ten most influential psychotherapists.
Carl Rogers was rated as number one.

One of Rogers's techniques, the therapist
reflecting back said the patient's statement by
rephrasing it and asking the person "How do YOU
feel about that?" has become almost a caricature of

contemporary psychotherapy. Indeed, comedian Bob Newhart, who grew up in Rogers's hometown of Oak Park, Illinois, caricatured Rogers's style of therapy in his highly successful television sitcom, "The Bob Newhart Show." But much of what Rogers contributed to psychotherapeutic theory is both remarkably simple and refreshingly optimistic. Rogers trusted people to want, and to work toward, good mental health and stability.

Yet Rogers introduced a multitude of revolutionary concepts to psychotherapy. His terminology, developed during half a century of research, helped to change mental health treatment forever. Rogers pioneered the notion that the people he saw were not "patients" who were "sick" in a medical sense, but rather "clients," people seeking help with problems of living. Today, that change in labeling from "patients" to "clients" is embraced by nearly all psychotherapists. Rogers not only perceived human beings as being primarily competent and striving toward good health, but he also viewed human ills such as insanity, criminal behaviors, and war as aberrations, anomalies superimposed upon a basic, commonly held desire for good.

Everything in Rogers's scheme starts from one life-force, a power that Rogers calls the "actualizing tendency." This life-force also exists outside the human psyche, according to Rogers. The actualizing tendency is present in all forms of life—trees that grow out of the sides of rocky cliffs, violets that push their way up through cracks in a concrete sidewalk, and men and women who struggle against the odds to do good things or create great accomplishments such as timeless works of art. This actualizing tendency is even active in the ecosystems of the world. Rogers found this life-force in the forests he roamed and in the cornfields he worked in as a youth.

Rather than identifying persons as "sick" or fundamentally flawed from childhood as the Freudians did, Rogers was interested in how he and other mental health professionals could recognize the health in people. Mentally robust people, in Rogers's view, exist in the here and now, free of defense mechanisms that would make it difficult for them to accept reality as it is. Called "the quiet revolutionary," Rogers went where no mental health professional had been before. His 1942 innovation of the tape-recording of psychotherapeutic interviews was far ahead of his time, but this method has now become standard practice for those providing mental health services. Many of these remarkable taped interviews done by Rogers over the years have been donated to the American Academy of Psychotherapists' tape library. These invaluable teaching tools are available to therapists all over the world.

Rogers is the undisputed creator of the "nondirective" or "client-centered" approach to psychotherapy. His decades-long study of how care is provided to clients resulted in the creation of several totally new mental health therapy techniques. Looking at the classic, highly directive

Freudian model of therapy, Rogers noted in *On Becoming a Person,* "Unless I had a need to demonstrate my own cleverness and learning, I would do better to rely upon the client for the direction of movement." Rogers's message to the client was also far removed from what Freud had communicated. Paraphrased, Freud's message to his patients was: I will discover the unknown flaw, developed in your earliest childhood because of psychosexual conflicts. I will root it out of your ego, superego and/or id and thus I will make you better. Conversely, Carl Rogers told clients: "I can't solve any of your problems for you, but I can help you to solve your own problems, and doing that will make you better."

Rogers was also an active participant in the development of the intensive form of group therapy sometimes referred to as the "encounter group." He is one of the first mental health professionals to conduct research regarding the effectiveness of various forms of counseling. A shy man who often refused television interviews, Rogers appeared on film interviewing clients. In 1962 he, Gestalt therapist Fritz Perls, and rational-emotive therapist Albert Ellis all were filmed during separate therapy sessions with the same client for what became known as "The Gloria Film Series." In the 1970 Academy Award-winning film "Journey Into Self," Rogers also appeared leading an encounter group.

Additionally, Rogers was instrumental in changing who provided therapy to the mentally ill. What had once been the exclusive domain of psychiatrists and psychoanalysts expanded to include all of the counseling disciplines—even educators and the clergy. His work with schools and other social support systems that provided services to children at risk affected many of the helping professions. An educator himself, Rogers never lost interest in the field of education. From his early years, during which he counseled abused and neglected children, until his death Rogers developed innovative ideas for administering mental health treatment to youth.

The unbelievable abundance of written (and published) work created by Carl Rogers from his youth to old age resoundingly shows both his amazing physical stamina and his strong work ethic. From his early college years in the early 1920s until his death in 1987, Rogers, besides maintaining a flourishing practice and lecturing all over the country, published sixteen books and more than two hundred articles. His writings embraced nearly every possible aspect of his work and his life—from therapy to scientific research, education to social issues, personal reminiscences to philosophy. The variety of publications for which he wrote speaks to the wide audience Rogers reached. He wrote articles for magazines as divergent as *The Family* and *Camping Magazine* to the *Journal of Consulting Psychology.* Several of his books have sold more than one million copies, and there are more than 60 foreign-language translations of his works.

As one of the foremost figures in the field of humanistic psychology as propounded by Alfred

Adler, Abraham Maslow, and Karen Horney, Rogers expanded many of their theories to embrace an even larger audience—the world. With his unshakable belief in the inherent goodness of people, he was convinced that proper communication could potentially stop even war. Carl Rogers acted on behalf of his beliefs. In the last decade of his life, he traveled to Belfast in Northern Ireland to reconcile Protestants and Catholics, and to South Africa to facilitate communication between black and white inhabitants of that country. Back home in the United States, Rogers tried to improve the dialogue between health care providers and consumers. At 85 years of age, Rogers made his last trip, to Russia. A modest man, Rogers was amazed to see how many Russians knew of his work and had read his writings.

PRINCIPAL PUBLICATIONS

- *The Clinical Treatment of the Problem Child.* Boston: Houghton Mifflin, 1939.

- *Counseling and Psychotherapy: Newer Concepts in Practice.* Boston: Houghton Mifflin, 1942

- *Counseling with Returned Servicemen.* New York: McGraw-Hill, 1946.

- *Client-Centered Therapy: Its Current Practice, Implications, and Theory.* Boston: Houghton Mifflin, 1951.

- *Psychotherapy and Personality Change.* Chicago: University of Chicago Press, 1954.

- *On Becoming a Person.* Boston: Houghton Mifflin, 1961.

- *A Therapist's View of Personal Goals.* Wallingford, PA: Pendle Hill, 1965.

- *The Therapeutic Relationship and Its Impact.* Madison, WI: University of Wisconsin Press, 1967.

- *Person to Person: The Problem of Being Human, A New Trend in Psychology.* Lafayette, CA: Real People Press, 1967.

- *Freedom to Learn: A View of What Education Might Become.*

Columbus, OH: Macmillan, 1969.

- *Freedom to Learn: Studies of the Person.* Columbus, OH: Charles E. Merrill, 1969.

- *Carl Rogers on Encounter Groups.* New York: Harper and Row, 1970.

- *Becoming Partners: Marriage and Its Alternatives.* New York: Delacorte Press, 1972.

- *Carl Rogers on Personal Power.* New York: Dell Publishing, 1977.

- *A Way of Being.* New York: Houghton Mifflin, 1980.

- *Freedom to Learn for the Eighties.* New York: Prentice Hall, 1983.

Family and early years

The family into which Carl Rogers was born, according to Rogers' own description, could have posed for Grant Woods' "American Gothic," the somber portrait of two Puritanical-looking members of a nineteenth-century American Midwest farm family. But beyond his family's Bible-reading and work ethic, there seems to have been very little that was unique about the middle-class, middle-American beginnings of Carl Ransom Rogers. Oak Park, Illinois, also the birthplace of Ernest Hemingway, was a quiet suburb of Chicago when Carl Rogers was born on January 8, 1902. He was the fourth child of prosperous middle-class parents, preceded by two older brothers, Lester and Ross, and a sister, Margaret. His mother, Julia (Cushing) Rogers was descended from New England ancestors that had arrived in America on the Mayflower. She was a housewife, a highly pious Christian, and a strict disciplinarian who brought up her children to be both hard-working and God-fearing. Rogers' father, Walter Alexander Rogers, was equally devout, and a respected Chicago civil engineer. In 1901, the year before Carl was born, Walter Rogers and an associate began their own construction company that quickly met with success, assuring the family's prosperity. There would be two more children born into the Rogers family after Carl:

Walter Jr. and John.

Howard Kirschenbaum, one of Rogers's several biographers, describes him as "a rather sickly child—slight, shy, prone to tears, often the target of jokes and teasing by his older brothers." In his childhood, he was extremely close to his mother. He was a precocious child, considered gifted, but also sensitive and prone to daydreams. Before he was four years old, Carl had already been taught to read by his mother and older siblings, and was already reading books, especially the Bible stories his mother encouraged him to read before he went to kindergarten. Rogers was able to skip the first grade completely. Throughout his childhood, Carl Rogers was what we would term a "loner," with no close friends. This appears to be more a factor of family expectations than any isolative tendencies in Carl. As a means of teaching their children, Walter and Julia Rogers gave each child a province of responsibility from which they could earn money but for which they were expected to be accountable. Carl was in charge of the hens. He fed them, kept the henhouse clean, collected the eggs, and even kept records and made out bills. In return for his efforts, he could sell eggs to both his mother and the neighbors and keep the profits. Helen Elliot, his future wife, who first met him in grade school, remembered him as reluctantly heading for home after school to sell eggs while the other children played.

When Carl Rogers was 12, his father, who was comfortable financially and looking for new challenges, decided to fulfill a lifelong dream and become a farmer. He bought 300 acres in Glen Ellyn, a rural community about 30 miles west of Chicago. When Carl Rogers speaks of growing up on a farm, in some ways it is a slight misnomer. The residence Walter Rogers built for his family at Glen Ellyn was an estate, complete with eight bedrooms, five baths, and a clay tennis court. Yet despite the elegance of their home, the Rogers children were still expected to do the majority of the farm chores and both attend and do well in school. Rogers spent his teenage years working on that farm, developing the work ethic, independence, and self-discipline that would characterize the rest of his life. His Bible-reading mother was a strict disciplinarian who Rogers's older brother once described as "a person you didn't tell things to." Rogers early years have frequently been described as solitary but character-building. The majority of his younger years were spent in the company of his brothers. (Margaret, being several years older, is described as having felt more maternal than sisterly toward Carl.) Rogers's own description of himself as a teenager, as presented in his 1980 book, *A Way of Being,* speaks volumes: "My fantasies during that period were definitely bizarre, and probably would be classified as schizoid by a diagnostician, but fortunately I never came in contact with a psychologist."

Education and marriage

"I have come to love my books a great deal," Rogers wrote in his diary during the summer of

1919, the year he graduated from high school. He had received a 50-dollar graduation gift from his parents, and with that money Rogers bought a set of chess pieces, some toilet articles, and 22 books. That same summer, as he prepared to enter the University of Wisconsin in the fall, he also wrote: "I have had lots of time to think this summer and I feel that I have come much closer to God, tho(sic) there are thousands of things that still perplex and baffle me." That autumn Rogers followed a family tradition and began attending the University of Wisconsin, initially majoring in agriculture. This was consistent with what he had written in that same diary a few days earlier: "I fully intend to be a farmer." Away from home for the first time in his life and clearly undecided as to his life work, Rogers managed to sustain good marks, but grew less sure about an agrarian future. Increasingly, he became involved in the Young Men's Christian Association (YMCA) and other religious activities, encouraging young people to preach the gospel all over the world. From his diary entries, Rogers burned with an evangelical fervor during that time, but he could not quite bring himself to decide to become a minister.

At the University of Wisconsin, Rogers reestablished a connection from his earliest years: Helen Elliot was also attending school there. He had not seen her since the Rogers family had moved to Glen Ellyn, and now he found that she had grown into a young woman who was "tall, graceful and very attractive." A few tentative dates soon blossomed into a relationship, though Helen continued to date others as well. Due to Helen's interest in art, she left the university to attend the Chicago Academy of Fine Arts after her sophomore year, but the bond between them continued as they corresponded and saw each other as often as possible. Helen influenced Carl to take his first tentative steps away from his family's fundamentalist religious views. He learned to dance and play cards; he joined a fraternity and attended college parties—all activities frowned upon by his parents. There seems to be a difference between Carl and his siblings in the ways they viewed their parents. Carl believed that his mother "became more fundamentalist" as she grew older, while his brothers and sisters felt that after her initial disapproval of Carl's first two years in college, their mother eventually accepted the changes.

In 1921 an event occurred that was destined to change Carl Rogers's life. Rogers was selected as one of 10 youth delegates to represent the United States at the World Student Christian Federation (WSCF) conference to be held in Beijing, China. Typical of Rogers's then-inability to see himself in a positive light, for several years he believed that he was chosen only because his parents were financially comfortable enough to pay for his trip. Christian leaders involved in his selection later denied this, however, saying Rogers' intelligence, commitment, and enthusiasm were the deciding factors. In February of 1922, he and the others embarked on an experience that would prove to be remarkably alien and broadening for a boy raised on a farm in the Midwest. He had proposed marriage to

Helen before he left, but she asked him to wait. Some accounts state that Rogers's family strongly disapproved of Helen, but it is unclear if this was truly the case. They seemed more disapproving of Carl's indecision regarding his own life than of his love for Helen. Yet it is possible that they did object to the relationship. In *A Way of Being,* Rogers observed,

> I think the attitude toward persons outside our large family can be summed up schematically in this way: Other persons behave in dubious ways which we do not approve of in our family. Many of them play cards, go to movies, smoke, dance, drink, and engage in other activities, some unmentionable. So the best thing to do is to be tolerant of them, since they may not know better, but to keep away from any close communication with them.

Though the Beijing conference lasted for only a week, the WSCF voyage would also take Rogers and the others to Japan, Korea, and the Philippines, and it would keep them in Asia for over six months —from February into August. Rogers would remain nominally a Christian, but he viewed his experience in the East as a conversion of sorts because it opened up for him philosophies to which he had never been exposed. This trip to Asia also made Rogers aware of two other things that would stay in his mind and become part of him: seeing first-hand the suffering of poor and exploited people, and the similarity of all of nature. He would note that silk "lost considerable of its luster" after seeing the child labor that produced it, and the observations of nature he made while climbing Mount Fuji are quite impressive. These lessons would become part of both his psychological theories and his life's work. In Rogers's words, "I consider this a time when I achieved my psychological independence. In major ways I for the first time emancipated myself from the religious thinking of my parents, and realized that I could not go along with them." In fact, Rogers's relationship with his family would never be the same after he returned from Asia. In 1922 he also showed the beginnings of an ability that would lead him to become a prolific writer. Later that year, Rogers wrote about his Asian experience in an article entitled "An Experiment in Christian Internationalism" published in *The Intercollegian,* a magazine sponsored by the YMCA. This article would be his first successful attempt at writing for publication, but it would hardly be his last.

Though it was during this trip that Rogers first began to doubt the religious interpretations inculcated into him by his mother and others (for example, he began to question whether Jesus Christ truly was a deity or only a remarkable man, a question that horrified his parents), he still returned to the University of Wisconsin determined to become a minister. That August, after returning from China, Rogers also took a correspondence course in psychology. For the first time, he read psychologist William James' work, but he found it quite boring. Of his first psychology course, Rogers would later remember only having a long-distance argument with his professor as to whether dogs were capable of reason. Rogers states, "I was quite able to prove to my own satisfaction that my dog Shep was definitely able to solve difficult problems by reasoning." Rogers' education at the University of Wisconsin continued for his junior and senior years, and he then applied to the Union Theological Seminary in New York City, noted for its progressive and tolerant religious teachings. He was accepted there, and in 1924, following graduation, he and Helen Elliot surprised nearly everyone by marrying on August 28. Helen had chosen to give up her ambitions of becoming a commercial artist. Their honeymoon consisted of packing up everything they owned and moving to "the smallest flat" in New York City.

In the summer of 1924, part of Carl's study for the ministry included a brief stint as a pastor in a church in East Dorset, Vermont, an experience both Carl and Helen enjoyed. He noted "I found it absolutely impossible to make my sermons longer than twenty minutes, a fact that disturbed me but for which my congregation was doubtless thankful. . .". In East Dorset, Rogers also began to focus upon the multiple social problems that he observed even in a small Vermont village. He described alcoholics and psychotic people who lived there. (East Dorset also happens to have been the hometown of Bill Wilson, the founder of Alcoholics Anonymous.) For Rogers, this exposure led him to an increasing interest in psychology, and the beginnings of the process that would eventually move him across the street to

Columbia University. Consistent with its reputation as an open-minded school of religion, Union Seminary in 1926 offered a student-run course entitled "Why Am I Entering the Ministry?" Rogers immediately signed up for it. "Why Am I Entering the Ministry?" proved an excellent means of winnowing the theological school's student body. As Rogers states, the majority of the attendees "thought their way right out of religious work." During those stressful years of decisions and new responsibilities, Rogers first suffered from what would become a lifelong problem: a peptic ulcer, a medical condition he shared with several other Rogers family members and which Carl suspected was caused by repressing their anger. On March 17, 1926, Carl and Helen's first child David was born. Before the year was over, Rogers had indeed crossed the street to Columbia.

Rogers, thanks to his parents' teachings, had always been enterprising. While in college after the China trip, he had run a small but lucrative importing business, sending for items from the East and selling them in the United States. While at Union Theological Seminary, he had held down a part-time job in Christian youth counseling. But now, at Columbia and the father of a baby son, an income once again became necessary. It is interesting to note that even during those busy years of working on the M.A. he received in 1928, and the Ph.D. in psychotherapy he attained in 1931, Rogers still managed to support his family. In 1928 Rogers accepted a position in clinic work at the Rochester Child Study Center under the auspices of the Rochester Society for the Prevention of Cruelty to Children. He, Helen, and baby David moved to Rochester that summer, and in the autumn their second child, Natalie, was born. Rogers would continue to work as a clinician, and eventually as the director, of both the Rochester society and its clinic. During those years, Rogers became increasingly aware of other psychotherapeutic techniques and theories then in wide usage. The work of Otto Rank, who believed that people were inevitably caught in a battle between their "will to health" and "will to illness," would greatly influence Rogers. Rank's belief that therapy was designed to aid people in accepting themselves and liberating their "will to health" seems to echo what Rogers came to believe. Yet Rogers, ever the maverick, stated on many later occasions, "I never had a mentor. I think that, to an unusual degree, my work was born out of direct experience."

Rogers also continued to write during those years. He even managed to write and publish an article entitled "Intelligence as a Factor in Camping Activities" in conjunction with C.W. Carson for *Camping Magazine* in 1930. Always prolific, Rogers continued to produce an eclectic series of articles for various journals and publications throughout the thirties. Many of these involved his ideas about clinical case work with children and psychotherapy. *The Clinical Management of the Problem Child,* a 1939 book that received little attention from the world at large or the world of psychology, was Rogers's first effort at developing his ideas into a book. It contained the seeds of many of the innovative theories that Rogers would later introduce to the world of psychology. Beginning in 1938, and culminating in 1939, Rogers became embroiled in his first professional battle. The Rochester Clinic was reorganizing, and it was suggested that it should be headed by a psychiatrist, rather than a psychologist such as Rogers. The emerging conflict eventually was decided in Rogers's favor, with his appointment as the director of the program. This incident verified his self-assessment of being "capable of dogged determination in getting work done or in winning a fight."

Teaching years

Rogers was 38 years old when he was offered a full professorship at Ohio State University in 1940. In the years prior to his university appointment, Rogers had quietly felt increasingly frustrated with and opposed to the authoritarian notions that were being proposed by Sigmund Freud and his followers. The people the Freudians called "patients" were more and more seen as "clients" by Rogers—individuals who indeed had psychological problems, but were not "sick" in the classic sense. In 1942 Rogers published a book that had a major impact on the psychotherapeutic world, *Counseling and Psychotherapy: Newer Concepts in Practice.* This work contained the first-ever references to people as clients rather than as patients. Both during and after World War II, Rogers was also actively involved in the United Service Organization (USO), helping returning veterans to cope with the psychological trauma that they had experienced. As always, Rogers put the knowledge he had acquired in working with these returning veterans into a book he wrote in 1946, *Counseling with Returned Servicemen.* In 1944, he was elected president of the American Association for Applied Psychology, an organization he had helped to found.

Rogers remained at Ohio State University until 1945, when the University of Chicago offered him joint positions teaching and setting up a center for counseling located at the university. At Chicago, Rogers conducted much of the research for which he became world-famous. This work arose from a decade-long campaign by Rogers for to explore the efficacy of and find ways to improve the various forms of mental health treatment. Prior to Rogers' time, the psychoanalytic interview, then the most common form of treatment of mental disorders, was considered sacrosanct. Psychoanalysts simply did not provide what they considered "privileged" information, and there was no measure of how effective their treatment had been except for their own version of how therapy had gone. Rogers became the counseling center's first executive secretary and managed to obtain grant funding for the research he had so strongly advocated for nearly a decade.

That same year, Rogers's newfound credibility with psychologists was enhanced when he was elected president of the more venerable American Psychological Association. Oddly enough, Rogers himself did very little of the actual research for which he has become known. He certainly was responsible for obtaining the necessary funds and for encouraging his students, providing ideas and publishing the first scientific studies of psychotherapy. But for the most part, his graduate students did the actual research. Rogers was far less interested in personal recognition, however, than in getting the job done. He often perceived himself as a facilitator of others, and in this endeavor he was highly successful. He continued working at the University of Chicago throughout the 40s and into the early 50s. During these years, as his fame grew, hordes of students from all over the world jammed his classrooms to attend his lectures. It was said that as soon as one lecture-hall was filled to overflowing, the university would provide a larger one. But soon that hall, too, would be too small and another, even larger one would be needed. He was given the least popular times to teach, such as early Saturday mornings, but still the classes were full and spilling over into the corridors.

While teaching at the University of Chicago in 1951, Rogers wrote what would become his best-known works: *Client-Centered Therapy: Its Current Practice, Implications and Theory.* In this book, Rogers for the first time spelled out his evolving personality theory.

> With all his ambivalences, the client wants to grow, wants to mature, wants to face his problems and work them through. Accept and clarify his initial

expressions of feeling, and a fuller, deeper expression of feelings will follow. Accept and clarify these, and insight will follow. Accept and clarify these insights, and the client will begin to take positive actions in his life and develop self-acceptance, self-understanding, and the ability to deal with his own problems.

Rogers called his theory his "hypothesis." That hypothesis, put in its simplest terms, states that all human beings intrinsically have the power to guide their lives into modes that provide them with personal satisfaction and social usefulness. In Rogers' version of psychotherapy, people are freed to search for their own singular type of internal insight, common sense, and self-confidence.

His alma mater, Columbia University, honored Rogers with the Nicholas Murray Butler Silver Medal in 1955, and this prize was followed the next year by a special contribution award from the American Psychological Association honoring his research into psychotherapy. In 1957, 55-year-old Rogers was invited by his other alma mater, the University of Wisconsin, to return and teach there. He eagerly accepted the offer, but it was a decision he would soon regret. Returning to the school where his education had begun 37 years earlier, Rogers was totally unprepared for the discord he met there. In his words, he was beginning to wonder

What is a university, at this stage of my career, offering me? I realized that in my research it offered no particular help; in anything educational, I was forced to fit my beliefs into a totally alien mold; in stimulation, there was little from my colleagues because we were so far apart in thinking and in goals.

In 1963, disillusioned with what we commonly call higher learning—dissatisfied with faculty diagnostic, therapeutic, and educational policies, Rogers resigned from the University of Wisconsin. It appears that Rogers maintained his disaffection with the university educational process. Although he continued to give visiting lectures and received honors from many colleges, Rogers never again was affiliated with any one school of higher learning.

Perhaps a disagreement between Rogers and the head of the psychology department at Stanford University, as described by Rogers's good friend Hobart "Red" Thomas, best clarifies part of the problem Carl Rogers had with academia. "I don't give a good god damn what the diagnosis is," Rogers is quoted as snapping in response to some statement about diagnosis made by the Stanford psychologist. "If we devote a fraction of the time we spend in diagnostic conferences to being with that person, you wouldn't need the diagnosis." Most accounts, however, describe Rogers as a man who did not argue with people. "Red" Thomas said of him: "He didn't get into arguments. He would state his position very clearly, and would listen to your position. 'Can we learn from each other?' was his basic stance." But little did Rogers know when he left Wisconsin that he was headed for much more work and fame. He was elected a fellow at the Center for Advanced Study in the Behavioral Sciences in 1962, and did work with the Western Behavioral Sciences Institute in La Jolla, California, a group that studied ways to improve human relations.

Later years

Throughout his 60s and 70s, Rogers remained remarkably healthy and mentally alert. His problems with the University of Wisconsin and others in academia apparently did not adversely affect the esteem in which he was held. He received honorary doctorates from several universities on both sides of the Atlantic, and the American Humanist Association selected Rogers "Humanist of the Year" in 1964. In 1968, the 66-year-old Rogers and some of his colleagues left the Western Behavioral Sciences Institute and founded the Center for Studies of the Person. Despite the tremendous exposure to people the world over that Rogers had enjoyed for decades, he remained basically a rather shy man. His 1970 book, *On Encounter Groups,* was judged by its publisher Harper and Row to have mass-marketing appeal. The book company wanted to set up a television interview for him, but Rogers adamantly refused. "But one show would lead to another!" an incredulous publishing executive argued. "That's what I'm afraid of," Rogers is said to have replied. He lived in California, continuing to see clients in his flourishing practice and conduct scientific studies at La Jolla. Rogers remained a frequent lecturer and prolific writer. During the last two decades of his life, between 1964 and 1987, Rogers wrote and published over 120 articles, including many that were published posthumously. In addition, Carl Rogers completed his last two books, *A Way of Being* and *Freedom to Learn for the Eighties,* in the last decade of his life.

"I am not growing old, I am old and growing" was Rogers's statement in "Growing Old—or Older and Growing," published in the *Journal of Humanistic Psychology* in the autumn of 1980, six years before his death. The last years of Rogers's life were, in many ways, the most remarkable. Consistent with his long-held belief that most human problems stem from poor communication, Rogers expanded his scope to aid the world rather than individual psyches. There is no doubt that the precarious situation in which the planet and its billions of people found themselves in the early eighties had been weighing on Rogers's mind. In the autumn of 1982, he had written a piece for the *Journal of Humanistic Psychology* entitled, "A Psychologist Looks at Nuclear War: Its Threat, Its Possible Prevention." He would soon, in keeping with the principles he had embraced all of his life, be "putting his money where his mouth was" and trying to facilitate healthy communication between the various factions in the world.

"I'm Carl Rogers. How will we use our time together?" was a typical lead-in Rogers used when conducting groups. This opening statement encouraged people to be accountable for their own knowledge, and for their part in the group process. When Rogers spoke of power, he'd explain, "I'm not interested in power over anyone. What I want is influence, to influence you to become the best you can possibly be." These are the tenets that Rogers, the master of the encounter group, brought to conflicts all over the world. During the last decade of his life, Rogers, now in his eighties, managed to visit Belgium, China, Italy, Hungary, Mexico, Germany, Russia, Sweden, Finland, Japan, Austria, Venezuela, England, Kenya, Zimbabwe, Brazil, and South Africa. In every country that he visited, Rogers met with professionals and offered them the principles he'd spent a lifetime developing. In Latin America, Northern Ireland, South Africa, and eventually the Soviet Union, he attempted to facilitate dialogue that truly would make war-torn people "the best they could possibly be."

In Belfast, Northern Ireland, at the height of the troubles, he managed to get Protestant and Catholic leaders to meet and to have active communication for a period of several days. Over that time, the two dissenting sides came, as "Red" Thomas said, "to see each other as people." Rogers, with his usual penchant for electronic gadgets, videotaped these meetings. Sadly, both the Protestants and the Catholics attending these meetings did not want this video shown out of fear that their constituents would feel betrayed. In South Africa, Rogers met a black man named Cecil Bobibe. Bobibe today is the dean of students at a

South African college and utilizes Rogerian concepts in his counseling practice. When asked what it was that Rogers brought to South Africa that so influenced him, Bobibe stated, "It (Rogers's theory) gives one faith in who we are, and shows one how to find the essential humanity in the other, whoever they might be." Rogers's last trip was to Russia in 1986, where he is still revered for his ability to facilitate conflict resolution. Carl Rogers died of a heart attack in San Diego, California, on February 4, 1987. He was quoted as saying that his last few years were the best times of his life.

THEORIES

Carl Rogers and humanist psychology

Explanation Carl Rogers was not the sole creator of what Maslow called "the third force," humanist psychology. Freud's psychoanalytic theories were considered one force, and behavioral theories pioneered by Ivan Pavlov and B.F. Skinner were a second force. Abraham Maslow, Karen Horney, and Rogers expressed an optimism regarding the human state that neither Freud nor Skinner found to be possible—humanistic psychology, or the "third force." Freud observed that "our mind is no peacefully self-contained unity." Rather he compared the mind to "a mob, eager for enjoyment and destruction . . . to be held down forcibly by a prudent superior class." Rogers, however, believed it had taken him years to undo both his early religious upbringing and Freudian training in psychology classes at Columbia, both of which had presented human beings as being inherently evil. Rogers's own observations had shown him that people are decent; they care about the society they live in; they are capable of positive accomplishments; and they deserve to be trusted.

Early in his career, Rogers also discovered that he did not subscribe to other commonly held beliefs promulgated by Freud and his disciples; namely, that early experiences and relationships set in place fixed and inevitable mental processes leading to neurosis. Instead, Rogers seemed much more at home with the philosophy of the humanists who believed that people were capable of changing. As in all of his later work, Rogers developed the seeds of these humanistic notions from the experiences he derived in his work with abused and neglected children at the Institute for Child Guidance in the Rochester, New York area in the early days of his career. Working with these children helped Rogers see the tremendous impact of both the biology he would later write about and the negative experience of childhood on which Freud based his theories. Yet in the majority of cases, Rogers found in these young lives the hopeful, humanistic philosophy that would be his mantra for the next six decades.

Changing the labels of therapy

Rogers was one of the earliest adherents of what has been called "interactional psychology"; as a result, much of the philosophy ascribed to him less abstract, simpler, and more practical than the complex theories proposed by many of his peers. Interactional psychologists believe that a healthy psyche is the result of appropriate and beneficial communication between people. Rogers continually described how such interactions should be carried out if therapists are to help people. He also explained how psychology measures helping people, and perhaps most importantly, he re-evaluated what the goals of such therapy should be.

Rogers redefined everything: the description of the person seeking help, who could provide that help, what help was actually provided, and how such help was given.

Rogers did more than change terminology when he changed what patients were called. Rogers's "patients" became "clients"—persons who were in need of assistance in reaching their innate potential. This change in perception would have far-reaching implications, and it would make Rogers the father of client-centered psychotherapy. This practice of referring to clients would spread across the world, forever altering the way the psychology profession perceives people seeking help. This model would also, in keeping with Rogers's core beliefs, improve the self-esteem of the clients whom psychologists and psychiatrists saw in therapy. It would reinforce a belief Rogers shared with his colleagues Karen Horney, Abraham Maslow, and others: that there is an ever-present capacity within each of us that instinctively seeks mental health, stability, and beyond that, the fulfillment of our potential.

Rogers's use of the reflection technique in his therapy sessions has been one of the most-parodied facets of Rogerian therapy. Rogers believed that "reflection of feelings" was one of two necessary methods used toward accomplishing what Rogers calls release, the freeing of the client from the pent-up feelings. This reflection, together with simple acceptance had to be manifested in order for the client to feel free to open up and experience catharsis—the expression of feelings previously not expressed (or sometimes not even consciously felt). Both of these techniques are designed to provide the client with assurance that the therapist is attentively involved in the psychotherapy session and is accepting of what is being expressed by the client. A classic example of simple acceptance would be the therapist's response of "Yes, I see...." Reflection of feelings as Rogers practiced it was more complicated, however. The ability to listen completely and totally is demonstrated to the client by the therapist mirroring back, and restating, the emotions behind what the client says.

Example Rogers provides the example of reflection in this interaction with one of his students who is getting failing grades. The supposed purpose of the session for this student is to make Rogers take responsibility for the student's decision to tell his parents.

Student: "Oh, I don't know if they're going to sort of condemn me . . . in the past they've said, 'It's your fault. You don't have enough will power'. . ."

Rogers: "You feel that they will be unsympathetic and condemn you for your failures."

Student: "Well my—I'm pretty sure my father will . . . He hasn't been—he doesn't experience these things; he just doesn't know what it's like . . ."

Rogers: "You feel that he could never understand you?"

The session goes on to eventually bring forth the real problem—the student's animosity toward his father and feeling of shame that this man is his father.

Because of his focus upon interaction, many of Rogers's tenets regarding therapy bring the contact between client and therapist under a microscope with a far sharper and more distinct lens. Though libertarian in his approach, refusing to be handcuffed by any pre-set protocols developed by Freud or anyone else, Rogers still actively set standards for psychotherapy. For Rogers, a pioneer in developing a complete and cogent school of psychological theory, the rationale behind the method of treatment used always remained less important than the personal qualities that the therapist possessed and brought to each counseling session. Far more than other humanists, Rogers insisted on taking a long and hard look at the attitude that the therapist brings to the psychotherapeutic session and how this affects the person being treated.

Over the years, Rogers began to experience and discover certain requirements for success in treating people. Much of what he learned and taught to others resulted from his innovative use of technology. Rogers began tape-recording therapeutic interviews with clients in 1942, long before this became a standard practice for psychotherapists. Based on what he learned from this experience, Rogers was one of the first to elaborate certain capabilities a therapist must possess in order to help clients attain their treatment goals. Rogers was also among the first to make these theoretical requirements a part of what he called "his hypothesis" of mental health care.

Rogers believed any therapist must possess four qualities, which he describes as being "necessary and sufficient":

- Congruence, or genuineness and sincerity. The quality of congruence is quite similar to one of Rogers's criteria for being "a fully functioning person," which will be discussed in more depth under Rogers's self-actualizing tendency theory. In his or her dealings with the client, the congruent therapist must present himself or herself honestly at all costs. He or she does not have to be perfect, but the therapist should never give the client the impression that they are false or "gameplaying," defensive, or all-knowing.

- Empathy, the ability to feel accurately what it is that the client is expressing. Saying "I know how you feel" when the therapist actually has no idea how the person is feeling is not considered helpful by Rogers.

- Belief that the therapist also learns from the client. The therapist should be able to quietly listen, without interrupting, and be able to provide an exchange of ideas and feelings with the client.

- Unconditional positive regard, a genuine liking and acceptance of the clients as they are. It is not necessary for the therapist to agree with everything the person says or does, but he or she must be able to accept the client totally, without any reservations.

Example Everyone, at one time or another, has tried to express to someone else how they feel when some terrible tragedy has visited them. If, for example, the person lost their spouse in the World Trade Center on September 11, 2001, and the listener responds, "Yeah, I know just how you feel . . . a distant relative that I hardly knew died two years ago in Europe and I was really sad," probably neither sincerity nor empathy is present.

Rogers's theories not only redefined who received therapy and the requirements for the provision of psychotherapy, but they also revolutionized who could provide such counseling. Prior to Rogers, mental health services were almost exclusively delivered by psychiatrists or analysts trained in psychology. Rogers's criteria for psychotherapists, however, make no mention of medical degrees or the need to have personally experienced psychoanalysis. Rogers actively encouraged the involvement of others in the provision of counseling services. For the first time, this inclusion brought social workers, teachers, clergy, and other people into the counseling area of mental health care. These innovative ideas paled in comparison, however, to the other changes in treatment that were developed by Rogers.

Initially, Rogers called the type of psychotherapy that he provided "non-directive." He perceived the therapist as accompanying the client on their journey but not leading the way. Rogers eventually changed this description to "client-centered" psychotherapy. Rogers believed that this title accurately indicated what was and was not provided by him during therapy. Rogers called his therapy "supportive rather than reconstructive." Sessions would address the client's agenda, not that of the therapist. Rogerian therapy would eventually undergo one more name change, coming less from Rogers than from others. It would become known as "people-centered," due to its increasingly wide application in so many other aspects of the real world beyond psychology—in marriage and parental counseling, child guidance, education, and even leadership seminars.

From the start of his career, Rogers developed methods to test the effectiveness of his therapy; he would continue that effort throughout life. More than any of his peers, Rogers always tried to define what he and his client were trying to accomplish in psychotherapy. From his vast experience, he succeeded in outlining what the process of Rogerian psychotherapy should look like. These were the measures of success, the necessary and inevitable series of events that effective client-centered psychotherapy always followed.

Rogers's "people-centered" psychotherapeutic process includes all of the following steps:

- The person manifests a willingness to seek help. (Whether the person is able to identify this willingness or not, they show it by making an appointment with the psychotherapist for therapy.)

- The therapist outlines the scope of the assistance that will be provided to the client. It is made clear that the therapist does not have the answers to the client's problems, but assures the person that they have the capability, with the therapist's assistance, of finding their own answers to their problems.

- A warm, comforting, and safe environment is provided through the therapist's attitude. This encourages the client to freely assert both their feelings and insights about their problems.

- Negative feelings are identified for the client with the help of the therapist and are given free rein.

- When the negativity has been completely expressed, the therapist elicits the positive responses from the client that Rogers's experience had taught him would then be present.

- Both the negative and the ensuing positive feelings are recognized and accepted by the therapist.

- These six steps ultimately lead the client to insight into their problems. This insight is accompanied by new acceptance of self and self-understanding. New possibilities of action to solve the problem are brought forth.

- Positive actions to solve the problems and a decreased reliance on the help of the therapist occur.

Main points

- Rogers's hopeful, humanistic approach towards treating the mentally ill was born in the most unlikely of places—in his early experience working with abused and neglected children in upstate New York.

- Though Rogers was not the sole originator of the humanistic school of psychology, he added many important innovations to it; for example, that persons seeking help were "clients" rather than sick people, or "patients."

- Rogers was among the first to actually tape record therapeutic interviews for teaching purposes and to define what it was that he, as a psychotherapist, was trying to accomplish during psychotherapeutic sessions.

- Rogers developed eight criteria, or steps, listed above, for successful psychotherapy.

- Rogers believed that theory mattered less

than did technique and the qualities the therapist brought to the psychotherapeutic interview. He believed that there were four qualities necessary in order for someone to successfully perform psychotherapy: congruence, or sincerity; empathy; the ability to listen and learn from the client; and a genuine liking and acceptance of the client.

Example Rogers himself provided the best metaphor for the type of therapy he spent his life practicing. He said it was similar to teaching a child to ride a bicycle. Though the teacher may initially hold onto the bicycle to steady it, eventually, in order to actually teach the child to ride, the teacher must let go of the bicycle and let the child try to ride independently. The child may take spills, yet eventually he or she will learn to ride the bicycle unassisted.

Rogers' core of personality

Explanation: The actualizing tendency For Rogers, plants and human beings gravitated toward survival in similar ways. Rogers, who in his youth had observed the plants and animals on his father's farm, had overheard the experts his father had consulted regarding breeding, learned the proper feed and environmental conditions, and observed the phenomenon of an urge for survival over and over again. In fact, in his early writings he cited mushrooms and seaweed as good examples of life struggling to live under adverse circumstances. But then Rogers began to think beyond why living organisms attempt to obtain the necessities of life, such as oxygen to breathe, water, and food. He pondered why intangibles such as safety, love, and autonomy are also valued and sought by not only human beings, but by other species as well. What Rogers came to conclude was that all living things were endowed with a genetic ability, what he terms "the core tendency" or the "actualizing tendency." This tendency not only gifted all species with a life force that made them instinctively seek to survive, but it also spurred them to go beyond survival to make the best of whatever circumstances in which they found themselves.

Rogers took this biological theory even further. He came to believe that his actualizing tendency applied not only to individual species of life but to entire ecosystems. More intricate, diverse living things, he believed, had an increased capability at survival solely because of their diversity. For example, if one species within an ecosystem such as a large forest ceased to exist, Rogers reasoned that there are most likely other species present in the forest that will take over the necessary functions to help the woodland survive. This ecological variety provided the forest with the flexibility that makes it more apt to be successful in surviving. His rural younger years had made these observations not terribly surprising and probably not much different from the observations of Darwin and others. Then Rogers took his actualizing tendency to a far different area. He ascribed this same core tendency to human personality development.

In addition to aiding survival, this actualizing tendency provides living things with a built-in capacity, developed during evolution, to know which things are good for them and which are not. The five senses are one example. Most people will not eat moldy, odoriferous food because of its offensive appearance and smell, thus saving themselves from food poisoning. Conversely, many people are tempted by the sight of a crisp apple, fresh from the tree, and most will savor the apple as they eat it. Clearly not all cases of food poisoning would be fatal and not all apples will be nutritious, but still people tend to make these choices. Observation of this behavior convinced Rogers that animals, and even babies, left to their own devices, will instinctively choose food that is right for them and necessary for their development. In other words, living beings desire and enjoy the taste of those things that they need in order to live. Rogers called such discretion "organismic valuing," and he extended the notion far beyond food choices.

Main points

- Living things have within them an innate capacity for both survival and even to go beyond survival to make the best of their lives.

- This capacity is determined by genetic factors rather than by the society in which they live.

- All living beings, animal and human, seek abstract good things such as safety, affection, and autonomy.

- Diverse living things have a greater capability of survival because they have more varied capacities to carry out functions necessary both to survival and improving life.

- Species instinctively want and enjoy the things that are necessary for their survival and growth.

- These observations of the basic needs for survival and comfort have implications far beyond the biological world. The same principles apply to the psyche.

Examples The tree growing out of the side of a cliff or the violets growing through the crack in a sidewalk mentioned earlier are examples of life's inborn capacity and instinctual need for survival.

Wolves traveling in packs provide themselves with a necessary means of survival: strength in numbers. But the wolf pack also furnishes each creature in the group with a social milieu and relationships that are satisfying and believed to be necessary for wolves. Elephants in the wild have a similar need for, and live according to, a social structure.

The Irish potato famine is a good example of

non-diversity making survival less sure. Because only one crop, potatoes, was planted in the Ireland of the 1840s, a disease specific to the potato plants obliterated entire potato fields, eventually starving those who were dependent on the potato fields for their survival.

Expansion of the actualizing tendency to human personality

The more complex the living being, the more complicated are its desires for the abstract things that are coonsidered to be good. This complexity provides human beings with an additional form of this actualizing tendency: the ability to improve, to make themselves into better people. Rogers calls this process of becoming the best we can be "self-actualization."

This core tendency for self-actualization consists of three separate areas:

- The self: A person's sense of who he or she is. The self comes into being early in life, as the person becomes aware of himself or herself as a separate entity and becomes able to describe oneself as "I" or "me." This self includes the person's personal perception of things, but it is a subjective perception rather than an objective one.

- Positive regard: Love, acceptance, and approval. Rogers perceives this need for positive regard as one universally shared by all of humankind. Though it is a requirement that is important throughout life, Rogers believes that it is most essential during infancy.

- Positive self-regard: Self-esteem, or approval and acceptance emanating from within the person that becomes a part of the person's concept of themselves.

Unlike the actualizing tendency common to all life forms, Rogers believes self-actualization is not genetically predetermined. Instead, it results from parental and societal influences on the individual, and it can be altered by family, friends, and the larger society. This self-actualization is the basis of personality development in Rogers's theory, and he manages to keep it quite simple: his personality theory recognizes only two divisions—those people whose self-actualizing capacity is active and fully functioning, and those in whom it not. In its most positive sense, self-actualization is why individuals attempt to make scientific discoveries, explore outer space, or attempt other creative endeavors. In many ways, Rogers seems more interested in describing what mental health is and how it is manifested than in looking at pathology. For Rogers, a person whose self-actualization tendency is fully functioning is a mentally healthy person, what he would call a "fully functioning person."

Rogers set up criteria that fully functioning persons would demonstrate. They are as follows:

- They would be open to the normal experience of life.

- They would be able to experience both pleasant and painful feelings that are appropriate reactions to the life situations they find themselves involved in.

- They would not use unsuitable or ineffective defense mechanisms.

- They would live existentially, that is, in the day or moment. (This does not imply that past experience is not used, only that the person uses their experience and lives in the present.)

- They would not respond with rigidity to situations. Similar to the forest described earlier, they would instead be spontaneous and able to adapt to change.

- They would possess positive self-regard, or self-esteem.

- They would have what Rogers would call "organismic trusting," that is, the ability to accept information, including experience and intuition, and trust that such information is right. Rogers values experience and intuition as being the most important. In Rogers's belief, if it feels right to the individual, it probably is right for that individual.

- They would operate with "experiential freedom": the ability to choose the most appropriate choice, based upon their experience.

- They would possess creativity, possessing a capacity for both thinking innovative and effectual thoughts and using these thoughts to produce innovative and effectual creations.

The fully functioning person probably represents a minority of the world's population, but Rogers truly believed that all people had within them the capacity for reaching this state of being. These fully functioning persons would be ones whose actualizing tendency and self-actualization would never have been thwarted by the world around them. They would have received positive regard from both parents and society as a whole, and therefore they would have developed positive self-regard. This ideal set of circumstances would lead them to what Rogers calls the "real self," the person who has achieved being both completely themselves and mentally healthy.

Main points In human beings, the actualizing tendency has another component: self-actualization. Self-actualization has three parts: The self (the ability to recognize oneself as an individual entity, similar to Freud's ego); the need for positive regard (the need, common to all humans, for acceptance, love, and approval); and the need for positive self-regard (the individual's internal acceptance and approval of self, leading to a positive self-concept, or self-esteem). Unlike the actualizing tendency, which is genetic, self-actualization is driven by the society in which one lives.

Rogers's personality development describes only persons for whom the self-actualizing tendency is operative and those for whom it is not. Persons with an actively functioning self-actualizing tendency are described by Rogers as fully functioning persons. Among the characteristics fully functioning persons share are openness, an ability to live in the moment, a capacity to trust both intuition and experience, freedom to make choices, and the competence to be creative. Becoming the "real self," a fully functioning person faithful to their own ideals and aspirations, is the true goal of Rogers's psychotherapy.

Examples The classic example of "the self" being subjective and dictated by the society one lives in is the young girl who has been told continually by an abusive parent that she is not pretty or that she is stupid. No matter how physically attractive she might be, or how high her IQ actually is, she will most likely continue to perceive herself as both ugly and stupid.

The need for positive regard was probably best described by a study done by researcher Rene Spitz decades ago in a South American orphanage. Some of the babies at the orphanage were not touched, held, or cuddled as babies would normally be. Eventually the babies from whom affection was withheld were noted to be failing. They died at a higher rate than infants that were given normal warmth and affection, indicating that the need for love is indeed both a psychological and physiological need.

The need for positive self-regard is basically the need to like and accept oneself. Many self-help groups address this need. One example is Al Anon, the worldwide support group for the loved ones of alcoholics and substance abusers. Al Anon literature contains 17 separate readings devoted to the subject of self-esteem.

When self-actualization isn't functioning

Explanation Though self-actualization should be based on the inborn abilities a person possesses, it is actually very much affected by upbringing and society. Therefore, the innate potential a person has may not always be manifested if forces outside of the person harm or attempt to destroy him or her. Rogers considers one of the most important negative forces to be conditional positive regard, or withholding of love, acceptance, and approval to the child by parents unless the child complies with the parents' expectations or wishes.

Society, too, plays its role in thwarting a person's self-actualization. All of the external forces a person meets in life—family members, teachers, clergy, political leaders, even the media—send the message that the person's needs will be met only if they conform to society's expectations. In theory, how closely we conform to these expectations will determine whether or not we get the rewards society has to offer. This message, Rogers states, provides all of us with "conditions of worth."

When conditional positive regard and conditions of worth provide the framework for a person's personality development, these factors, viewed as negatives by Rogers, will eventually be internalized, leading to what he calls "conditional positive self regard," or self-esteem based solely on meeting other people's expectations. The individual will become reprogrammed to fashion themselves into an entity that is pleasing to parents and society at large, but not to themselves. Organismic valuing and experiential freedom, the basic building blocks of decision-making that lead to good mental health, will be abandoned.

Conditional positive self regard leads to the development of an "ideal self," Rogers believes. In his lexicon, "ideal" does not mean something positive, but rather a self that sets itself standards that are impossible to meet. This ideal self is an internally imposed goal that is always unattainable, and the notion leads to what Rogers calls "incongruity," and what the mental health movement prior to Rogers had called neurosis. If the real self could be described as what a person truly is, the ideal self could be characterized as what everyone else, and ultimately the person themselves, thinks they should be. The greater the difference between the real self and the ideal self, the greater the amount of mental distress that is present.

Rogers calls life events that clearly present the

incongruity between the real self and the ideal self "threatening situations." If people find themselves in a situation where they are expected to be competent and calm, such as giving a speech, and instead they feel terrified, they will experience anxiety. The feeling of anxiety is a physiological response to mental discomfort, a signal that the person should physically escape from the uncomfortable predicament and run away as fast as possible. Quite often, however, people still have to do things that make them feel uncomfortable. Therefore, they develop psychological escape mechanisms that are referred to in psychology as defenses. If the person cannot run away in the physical sense, then they instead run away within their psyche.

Rogers believed that all defense mechanisms are completely based on perception, or how the person views an anxiety-producing situation. He recognizes only two defense mechanisms: denial and perceptual distortion. Rogers's denial is quite similar to Freudian denial. Rogerian denial gives the individual the capacity to completely obliterate (or deny) the existence of an unpleasant, stressful fact. Rogers's denial also includes Freudian repression, or refusal to allow the anxiety-producing thought to come into the consciousness. Perceptual distortion occurs when an individual acknowledges an anxiety-producing reality, but then (unrealistically) re-interprets it to diminish its capacity for causing stress.

According to Rogers, all human beings use

defense mechanisms to some degree. The more defense mechanisms that a person employs, the less the real self is operational within the person. This leads to an even wider differentiation between the ideal self and the real self. This in turn results in an increase in incongruence, or neurosis. Rogers sees psychosis as merely an extension of this theory. When the person's defense mechanisms become completely overwhelmed, all sense of self—both real and idealized—becomes severely damaged; the psychotic person loses the ability to distinguish between the self and others.

Rogers set up similar criteria to describe the maladjusted person:

- The person lives defensively and would not be open to experiencing either pleasant and painful feelings.

- The person's life goals are based on a plan developed by someone else, perhaps the person's parents or society.

- The person does not utilize either organismic trusting or intuition.

- The person feels that they were not free to make choices and feels manipulated by others.

- The person would be unimaginative and conform to commonly held conceptions, whether these were right or wrong.

Main points

Self-actualization does not develop as it is naturally intended when forces outside of the person interfere with it. Rogers believed that if parents offered their child love, acceptance, and approval only if he or she met the parents' expectations, in his words, "conditional positive regard," that child would encounter significant road-blocks in reaching self-actualization. What Rogers called "conditions of worth," or demands put onto the person by society at large, require that the person conform to the expectations of family members, teachers, clergy, and the media, in order to receive positive things as rewards. People programmed by conditional positive regard and conditions of worth will eventually internalize these conditions for acceptance, creating conditional positive self-regard, or self-esteem entirely based upon living up to others' views of what they should be. This situation eliminates organismic valuing and experiential freedom from the decision-making process, alienating the person from their true self and from good mental health.

Conditional positive self-regard aids in the development of an ideal self, one that imposes impossible, unattainable demands upon the person. These demands, and the distance between this ideal self (what the person is conditioned to think they should be) and the real self (what the person really is) produce what Rogers calls incongruity, or neurosis. The size of the gap between the real self and the ideal self, indicates the degree of incongruity or neurosis that is present. Those events that make evident the incongruity between the real self and the ideal self are called by Rogers "threatening situations," which lead to anxiety. Anxiety produces a physiological response that calls for the person to run away from the threatening situation. When a person cannot in reality run away from a threatening situation, they run away within their mind by using defense mechanisms.

For Rogers, there are only two defense mechanisms: denial and perceptual distortion. These defenses are based entirely upon the person's perception. Rogers's version of denial is similar to Freud's, but it also includes repression. Perceptual distortion is the re-interpretation of reality to make it less stressful. The use of defense mechanisms to some degree is a universal thing. The use of defense mechanisms makes the real self less functional, increasing the gap between real self and the ideal self. The greater this gap, the more what Rogers calls incongruence, or neurosis, that is present. For Rogers, psychosis is only an expansion of this theory, occurring when the person's defense mechanisms are completely breached and there is a shattering of both real and ideal self.

Examples Conditional positive regard is exemplified by the parents that show affection only when the child has done something that they perceive as being "good," such as washing their hands and face, and keeping their clothing immaculate while out playing. The child that comes in from playing covered with mud is then shouted at by the parents and treated in a rejecting manner.

Probably the most classic and mundane example of a condition of worth is the statement, "If you don't eat all your meat and vegetables, you cannot have dessert."

An overachiever who is never satisfied with his or her accomplishments is a person who has developed conditional positive self regard. This person's ideal self is so perfect that it is unattainable. Yet another example of a person with an ideal self is someone who wants her family to look perfect to the outside world no matter how upset and unhappy the family might actually be.

Gloria Swanson's character Norma Desmond, in the classic movie "Sunset Boulevard," exhibits several of Rogers's characteristics of a person living with an ideal self rather than a real self. Norma, a former great and beautiful movie actress, has grown old and is no longer attractive. Her ideal self is still young, beautiful, and successful in films. When reality makes her look at the actual substance of her situation, she uses denial (she is still beautiful and desirable) and perceptual distortion (everyone is jealous of her) to avoid reality. Norma Desmond eventually goes beyond incongruence, or neurosis, into psychosis.

HISTORICAL CONTEXT

When he wrote his landmark book, *Medical Inquiries and Observations upon the Diseases of the Mind,* in 1812, Philadelphia physician Benjamin Rush could not have known that he would one day become known as "the father of American psychiatry." Rush, a pious and charitable Pennsylvania physician, had advocated for some time for better treatment of the mentally ill. When he wrote his book, he was 67 years of age, and he had lived through enough adventure to fill several lifetimes. An early fighter against slavery, a patriot in the Revolutionary War, and a signer of the Declaration of Independence, Rush's battle to defeat the great yellow fever epidemic of 1793 in the United States' then-capitol, Philadelphia, probably earned him more fame and controversy in his lifetime than the book he wrote just one year before he died.

In fact, much of the controversy surrounding Benjamin Rush had nothing to do with psychiatry. He was a strong believer in the popular remedy of "bleeding" people, regardless of their diagnosis; many of his colleagues in Philadelphia, however, disagreed with his use of bleeding as a treatment for yellow fever. It is unknown if his blood-letting of mentally ill persons caused any debate. Certainly his observations regarding "Diseases of the Mind" evoked little stir. Yet Rush's book brought new thinking to an America that was considered a primitive, uncivilized backwater. Rush's observations closely mirrored those of fellow physicians Phillipe Pinel in France and Quaker William Tuke in England, who both advocated enlightened and more humane treatment for the mentally ill. Unfortunately Rush's book was flawed in two ways. It leaned heavily on astrology, a belief common in his time. But more important, it also subscribed to one of the two false theories about the cause of mental illness then in vogue: that mental illness, or "madness" as it was then called, was the result of a problem with the arteries supplying the brain with blood, causing inflammation. (The other then-popular theory was that sin caused mental illness; Rush apparently did not subscribe to this notion.) Besides his book, Rush also influenced American mental health through his invention of "the tranquilizer," a restraint that eerily resembles the electric chair. It was not as cruel as it looks, from all reports, and it was designed to decrease blood circulation to the brain.

In 1827, Thomas Upham published what is considered the first textbook of psychology: *Elements of Intellectual Philosophy*. Like Benjamin Rush's observations, Upham's book would do little to improve the quality of life for people suffering from psychiatric problems. But 30 years after Rush's death, a woman named Dorothea Dix would have appreciably more impact upon psychiatric treatment. A Massachusetts school mistress, Dix would shame Commonwealth politicians and sheriffs when she convincingly argued that the people with psychiatric illnesses in Massachusetts jails, contrary to what was then widely believed, really did feel the cold when they were shackled naked to beds in unheated cells in the dead of winter.

> I proceed, gentlemen, briefly to call your attention to the present state of Insane Persons confined within this Commonwealth, in cages, closets, stalls, pens! Chained, naked, beaten with rods, and lashed into obedience!

Dix's 1843 "Memorial to the Massachusetts Legislature" would eventually raise millions of dollars and create 32 mental hospitals in 20 states across the United States and in two Canadian provinces. Dix's castle-like stone hospitals, turreted and sitting atop hills away from the rest of the populace of cities and towns, at least provided kinder and better care for the mentally ill. They also came to be landmarks across the country. At first the medical profession had little to do with these "asylums," but gradually psychiatric care came to be seen as a specialty of medicine, and physician-superintendents became the norm. In 1844, the Association of Medical Superintendents of American Institutions for the Insane came into being.

For most Americans, psychiatric illness continued to be something both mysterious and frightening. These physicians that locked up the mentally ill in fortress-like hospitals as far removed as possible from the community did little to educate the public concerning the nature of mental illness. That lack of public education was primarily the result of a lack of knowledge. Neither Benjamin Rush, Thomas Upham, the hospital superintendents, nor Dorothea Dix really understood the causes or the effects or the treatment of emotional problems. Even as late as the Civil War, some doctors still subscribed to Rush's circulation-to-the-brain theory, while others adamantly believed mental illness was a result of wrongdoing. Harvard professor William James became America's first modern psychologist in 1890 when he wrote and published *Principles of Psychology.* The American Psychological Association came into being in 1892. In the same years, American psychologist E. L. Thorndike's studies of laboratory animals produced some of the earliest information on conditioned responses, work that Thorndike hoped to apply to education. But, echoing Dix decades earlier, it would take another layperson to give the public the first shreds of useful information regarding mental illness.

Clifford Beers was an articulate and intelligent Yale graduate who suffered from bipolar disorder, then called manic-depressive illness. Shortly after his graduation from college in the early 1900s, he suffered a mental collapse that resulted in his being hospitalized in several of what were then called "mental asylums." Though much of the neglect and mistreatment of patients common in Dix's time had been eliminated, Beers soon discovered that confining patients in strait-jackets and choking them into unconsciousness were still very much a part of mental health care in American psychiatric hospitals. Beer's mistreatment and his recovery in spite of it became the basis of his 1908 bestseller, *A Mind that Found Itself.* Two of Beers' staunchest and most influential admirers turned out to be James and famed psychiatrist Adolph Meyer. Meyer coined a new name for what was then commonly called "madness"—"mental hygiene." That same year, the Society for Mental Hygiene was founded, soon followed by a National Committee for Mental Hygiene, an organization that became international in 1919.

German education, especially regarding the study of the new-found science of psychology, was considered the best in the world at the beginning of the twentieth century. It was quite common for American students interested in the study of the mind to attend school in Europe, preferably in Germany. Wilhelm Wundt had established the first psychology laboratory at Leipzig, Germany in 1879, and American psychologist G. Stanley Hall was impressed enough with the German model to establish the first American psychology laboratory at Johns Hopkins Hospital in Maryland the next year. Hall moved on to Clark University in Worcester, Massachusetts, where he incorporated the German concept of graduate education. Hall's interest in psychology led to his inviting Sigmund Freud and Carl Jung to lecture at Clark in 1909, Freud's only trip to the United States, and one that deeply influenced American psychological thought. The first psychological studies of learning, with rats negotiating mazes, occurred at Clark University under Hall's auspices, and he was an early pioneer in the field of psychological studies regarding children.

For the majority of mentally ill Americans in the early twentieth century, however, neither psychiatry nor psychology significantly improved their treatment. In fact, both areas of learning remained the exclusive domain of intellectuals that shared their findings only among themselves. Furthermore, most practitioners of the newly discovered science of psychology discriminated against women. Three American women psychologists faced overwhelming sexual discrimination in the early years of the twentieth century, yet Mary Whiton Calkins, Christine Ladd-Franklin, and Margaret Washburn all managed to make major research contributions in their field. Calkins was banned from graduation from Harvard University, even though she had taken classes there, had passed all her courses, and was considered one of the university's most brilliant students. Both Ladd-Franklin and Washburn also were victimized by discriminatory practices several times during their careers. Yet, with incredible effort, these three women still managed to leave a lasting impression on American psychology. Calkins developed a memory procedure that is still used today, and she was the first woman president of the American Psychological Association. Ladd-Franklin was responsible for an evolutionary theory regarding color vision, and Washburn did impressive work in the field of comparative psychology.

Gender bias ran rampant within both

psychiatry and psychology. American psychologist E.B. Titchener, who was educated in Germany, returned to his native country to write a 1909 book called *Titchener's Textbook of Psychology* and initiated the psychological approach known as structuralism. To pursue his passion for psychological research, he led a group of male-only researchers that called themselves "experimentalists." Both Columbia University and the University of Chicago, schools that would later employ Rogers, became quite active in the development of psychology in the United States, but neither school did much to encourage women's participation, educate the public regarding mental illness, or actually help troubled people. An example of one of the very few understandable public statements regarding psychological theory was made by James Angell, one of the first presidents of the American Psychological Association. Two schools of psychology had developed within American universities: the previously mentioned structuralism and another called functionalism. Angell explained the difference between the two schools of thought this way: "Structuralists ask, 'What is consciousness?' while functionalists ask, 'What is consciousness for?'" Few of his contemporaries made things as simple.

Despite its researchers' lack of communication with most of the American public, psychology became an important component of higher education. Mental testing for educational purposes was among the earliest psychological testing to have been developed and employed in the United States, but unfortunately it quickly proved to be flawed. Henry Goddard (the originator of the term "moron") brought European intelligence testing to America. Alfred Binet's methodology had originally been developed to identify academically weaker students so that special programs could be developed to help them learn. Unfortunately, these early Binet tests were perverted and used to discriminate against certain Southern and Eastern European immigrants who came to America during the early years of the twentieth century. Eventually, this mode of testing developed into a more useful form, the Stanford-Binet IQ test, which is still used today. But in spite of these small steps forward, neither psychology nor psychiatry in the early twentieth century seemed capable of developing or carrying out concepts that would improve life for people with mental illness. Psychology had an image of rats in mazes or of flawed tests that proved skewed racial theories rather than a field that could help human beings. It would take Carl Rogers and others like him to put a more human face on the field of psychology.

CRITICAL RESPONSE

Disfavor among academics and parts of society

The contrast between Rogers's strong positive impact on clinical psychology in the real world and the lack of regard he enjoys among psychology professors in academia is impressive. Biographers Howard Kirschenbaum and Valerie Henderson note in their 1989 book, *The Carl Rogers Reader,* that

> Rogers spent his whole life not only asserting the importance of the democratic and libertarian ideal in all human relationships, but seeking ways to accomplish that ideal. He innovated, he described, he modeled, he even proselytized. For that he won hundreds of thousands of appreciative students whose work touches millions of lives each year....he also won thousands of influential critics who have prevented Carl Rogers and the people-centered approach from becoming the mainstay of professional training in the academic institutions of the United States.

Yet, as noted previously, a 1982 study conducted by the American Psychology Association that polled practicing psychologists and psychotherapists ranked Rogers first in a rating of "The Ten Most Influential Psychotherapists."

Kirschenbaum and Henderson go on to state that "not all professionals have been pleased with Rogers's influence. Many find his theory and methods oversimplified. Others argue that trusting the individual's resources for self-help will not work and might even do harm." Psychologist and college professor C. George Boeree investigates this criticism in more detail. He refers to Rogers's "organismic trusting" as "a major sticking point" in Rogers's theories—not only for academics but also for those lay persons with a fundamentalist ethos. If the definition of organismic trusting is, as Rogers would say, having faith in ourselves that if we do what feels naturally right it will prove to be the right thing to do, it becomes clear that this could indeed become a slippery slope. To paraphrase Dr. Boeree, this could mean that if you are a sadist, you should hurt other people; masochists should hurt themselves; if you like drugs or alcohol, go for it; and if you're feeling depressed, kill yourself. This "If it feels good, do it!" attitude, often expressed by young adults but criticized by society at large during the 60s and 70s, has frequently been blamed on Rogers. Dr. Boeree further reflects, however, that organismic trusting would of necessity be in keeping with knowledge of the real self; consequently, by Rogers's definition, the real self would most likely not be compatible with sadism, masochism, substance abuse, or severe depression.

Rogerian therapy also often faced ridicule

based upon its use of reflection of feelings. Rogers always said that the ability of the therapist was the most important facet of any Rogerian psychotherapy; still, there were those who believed that they were following Rogers's tenets but actually were not. Two common anecdotes prevalent among the psychological community in the 1950s, as reported by Howard Kirschenbaum in his earlier (1979) book *On Becoming Carl Rogers,* illustrate the common perception and criticism:

> I once went to a Rogerian counselor. I started talking about my problems and all he did was repeat back, word for word, everything I said. I couldn't figure out who was the crazy one, him or me. I said, I know that. That's what I just told you. So he said, You know that. That's what you just told me. After a while, I started getting really angry. So then he tells me I'm getting angry.

The following anecdote is both frightening, darkly humorous, and totally untrue. However, this mocking spoof of Rogers's type of therapy was a particular favorite of his critics during those years. It describes a fictional client's interaction with Carl Rogers during an appointment with Dr. Rogers in his office, on the 34th floor.

Client: "Dr. Rogers, I've been feeling awfully depressed lately."

Rogers: "Oh, you've been feeling very depressed lately?"

Client: "Yes, I've even seriously been considering suicide."

Rogers: "You feel you might like to kill yourself."

Client: "Yes, in fact I'm going to walk over to the window here."

Rogers: "Uhumm, you're walking over to the window there."

Client: "Yes, I'm opening the window, Dr. Rogers."

Rogers: "I see. You're opening the window."

Client: "I'm about to jump."

Rogers: "Uhumm. You're about to jump."

Client: "Here I goooooo.... ." (the client jumps).

Rogers: "There you go."

A loud crash is heard below. Dr. Rogers walks over to the office window, looks down, and says, "Splat!"

But perhaps the bias against Rogers's tenets arises not just from the prejudice of intellectuals or society's fear of pleasure-seeking and self-indulgence, but rather from Western culture's love affair with technology. Kirschenbaum and Henderson further observe in *The Carl Rogers Reader,* that "Rogers's message points us in a different direction (from technology)....what really matters is trust in ourselves and others, in communication, in how we handle our feelings and conflicts, in how we find meaning in our lives." They note that it is not only the professors in universities who have resisted Rogers's body of work. Ironically, it seems that the man who was such an innovator in the use of the twentieth century's gadgets—tape recordings, films and other media—is also the victim of society's fascination with this same technology. As a humanist, Rogers's belief in good communication and understanding between people is, in the end, more difficult and takes longer than technology's quick fixes. Rogers leads people away from computer programs, pills that provide chemical solutions to behavioral problems, and all the other proposed technocratic solutions to humanity's woes.

Rogers's common ground with other humanist psychologists

Humanistic philosophy of mental health treatment can be defined in many different ways. Most experts generally agree, however, that it includes three commonly held tenets: the importance of the person's perception of reality; the importance of helping people to understand both the significance and the definition of good mental health; and the need to encourage humanness and the ability to choose. Based on those criteria, it is clear that Rogers qualifies as a humanist. But going beyond the label, if often appears that the differences between Rogers and other humanist psychologists are more a matter of terminology than actual philosophical differences. Whether referred to as the actualization tendency by Rogers, self-realization by German-American psychoanalyst Karen Horney, or self-actualization by Abraham Maslow, the notion that human beings possess both an inborn desire for mental health and the capacity to realize that health is the common thread among the humanists.

Rogers' "conditional positive self regard," or the development of a person's self-esteem that is based on complying with the requirements of others, is remarkably similar to the theory propounded by Karen Horney. As did Horney, Rogers believes that this society-induced betrayal of the self is one of the building-blocks for the development of neurosis, or what Rogers called incongruence. The conditional regard of parents as described by Rogers is quite similar to the basic evil as described by Horney: parental indifference unless the child complies with their wishes. Maslow's "hierarchy of needs," progressing from basic physiological requirements such as hunger, thirst, and sex to self-actualization is very similar to Rogers' transition from the "actualizing tendency" to the "fully functioning person."

It is worth noting, however, that Rogers, humanist though he was, did not actually describe human beings as being basically good. In his 1977 book *A Way of Being,* Rogers explained his theory, as he so often did, in terms of a remembered perception from his teenage farming years. He talks about the family's winter storage of potatoes in a bin in the cellar, a few feet from a window. As spring approached and the light and temperature increased, these potatoes would put forth white, spindly shoots reaching toward that window. These sprouts would be totally different from the healthy green growth that a potato would put forth when planted in the rich soil outdoors. These unhealthy buds, reaching toward the light, though they would not be destined to flourish, would also not give up. Rogers noted that these potato sprouts made him think of

> clients whose lives had been terribly warped . . . men and women on back wards of state hospitals. So unfavorable have been the conditions in which these people have developed that their lives often seem abnormal, twisted, scarcely human. Yet the directional tendency in them (the wish to be mentally healthy) is to be trusted.

Yet Rogers surely did share with other humanists their disagreement with Freud's conception of the inherent malevolence of the human race. He addressed this contention, specific to the Freudian beliefs of famed psychiatrist Karl Menninger, in Rogers's article, "A Note on the Nature of Man," published in the *Journal of Counseling Psychology* in 1957. Menninger had reportedly told Rogers that he viewed man as being "innately destructive," a premise that made Rogers "shake his head in wonderment." In the article,

Rogers looked to the animal world for comparison regarding inborn characteristics, believing that most people have fewer preconceived prejudices there. He described the lion, often perceived by people as being a "ravening beast," as in reality a well-adjusted creature. He noted that in their natural habitat lions kill only for food, are never gluttonous, and do not become obese. Furthermore, most lions develop into mature, independent, and self-responsible creatures that care for their young and understand about working cooperatively to survive. Similarly, Rogers stated that the human beings he had counseled had taught him that

> to discover that an individual is truly and deeply a unique member of the human species is not a discovery to excite horror. Rather I am inclined to believe that fully to be a human being is . . . [to be] one of the most widely sensitive, responsive, creative and adaptive creatures on this planet.

Relationship to Gestalt therapy

Freud and his disciples tend to look at their patients from the outside inward, trying to understand their patients' distorted view of reality. Conversely, Gestalt therapists do their best to go inside their patients and look outward, viewing the world from the person's internal vision of things. Early in the twentieth century, prior to World War I, German psychologists Max Wertheimer, Wolfgang

Kohler, and Kurt Koffka began to perform experiments on monkeys and other animals and apply the results to human beings. In one experiment, researchers placed a banana (the reward) in an unreachable but visible place outside of the laboratory monkey's cage. If the monkey was given a sufficient number of sticks, Gestalt researchers learned that the creature would figure out how to assemble the sticks in order to successfully get hold of the banana. This outcome made Gestalt therapists believe that human beings, too, were innately capable of reasoning their way toward goals or solving problems. This belief is quite similar to Rogers's self-actualizing tendency.

Debates with behaviorist B.F. Skinner

In the late nineteenth century, American psychologist E.L. Thorndike began laboratory work that produced some of the earliest information on conditioned responses. Thorndike's interest was primarily in regard to education. In the early twentieth century in Czarist Russia, a psychologist named Ivan Petrovich Pavlov was also conducting animal research that showed the ability to produce emotional states by repeated conditioning. Thorndike and Pavlov's research was the beginning of behaviorist psychology, but most Western psychologists initially were unaware of Pavlov's contributions, as his work was not translated in the West until 1920. This research led to B.F. Skinner's efforts in the 1930s. The basic premise behind Skinner's research was that the more a certain behavioral response was rewarded, or "reinforced," the more that response was likely to happen again. This principle, called "operant conditioning" by Skinner, became the most common and popular version of behavioral psychology.

Skinner would take this notion even further, into political and social spheres, in his novel, *Walden Two.* This book proposed a utopian society that would be populated by ideal people who would be created as a result of operant conditioning. These Walden Two inhabitants would be mentally healthy, productive, and happy, and thus they would no longer need such abstract concepts as democracy or capitalism because there would be no class struggles.

Rogers took issue with much of behaviorist theory. As early as 1946, he had noted that, although behavior could be determined by the external influences to which an organism is exposed, "it also may be determined by the creative and integrative insight of the organism itself." In 1956, Rogers and Skinner met for the first time to debate their differences at the American Psychological Association's annual convention. Two more debates took place in the early 1960s.

From most reports, there was no winner in any of the three debates. Both Rogers and Skinner were remarkably articulate and informed presenters of their positions. In nearly all of these discussions, Rogers brought up *Walden Two,* and at one point noted that he saw little difference between that book and George Orwell's science-fiction classic *1984,* wherein all people are conditioned by punishment to be the same and to obey a dictator known as "Big Brother." Though they met for only those three debates, the dispute between Rogerian libertarianism and behavioral conditioning has continued. Rogers' position is probably best expressed in a statement he wrote in 1947:

> Significant problems of social philosophy are also involved in these diverging attitudes regarding therapy. If objective study supports the conclusion that dependence, guidance and expert direction of the client's therapy and life are necessary . . . then a social philosophy of expert control is clearly implied. If further research indicates that the client has at least the latent ability to understand and guide himself, then a psychological basis for democracy would have been demonstrated.

THEORIES IN ACTION

For over 50 years, Rogers's work has continued to exert an major impact upon all aspects of psychology, and that impact has even spread far beyond the borders of what most people would term mental health. In nearly aspect of life in the twenty-first century, his legacy continues. His beliefs have influenced diverse groups, such as teachers, motivational speakers, and social workers. Rogers's encounter group ideas have been applied by both Rogers himself and others in efforts to bring about peace within communities and throughout the world. The multitudes of groups that try to discover each others' humanness and thus defuse ignorance and hate are the direct result of Rogers's ideas. The specific group discussions that Rogers facilitated in Northern Ireland and South Africa are examples of this, as are community groups in poor, urban areas that meet regularly with local police to discuss problems and feelings.

Research

Rogers worried from the beginning that Rogerian therapy could become dogmatic, as had other forms of psychotherapy and analysis. (The best example of this dogmatism would be Freudian theory.) Increasingly, Rogers became convinced that "psychotherapy may become a science, applied with art, rather than an art which has made some pretense of being a science." The only way that psychotherapy could be a science would be through research, developing measures of the success of psychotherapy sessions. From the beginning of his practice and writing in the 1930s, Rogers advocated for the inclusion of such study. What made the research possible was Rogers's tape-recording of his client's psychotherapeutic interviews, which he began in 1941. In the ten years that followed, Rogers would record more than 40 complete cases. By 1957, he had taped over 200.

The first phase of Rogers's research ran between 1940 and 1948. These studies were admittedly random and subjective, based on the ideas and needs of the individual researchers (usually graduate students) that worked with Rogers during those years. These investigations sought to identify what happened during therapy, measured how directive or non-directive the therapist was, tried to determine how much emotional expression and insight were developed by the client, and estimated how the researchers perceived the success of the therapy. There were a total of 13 of these early studies done, and these were considered by most to be merely explorations of Rogerian psychotherapy. Elias Porter, a student from Ohio State University, conducted and published the first of these studies in 1943. Based upon Rogers' often-repeated and published statements that the process and progress of therapy was a predictable thing, these graduate student researchers attempted to confirm or invalidate his vision of what happened in psychotherapy sessions. It was considered an exploratory form of research only, and it had obvious failings. Even if insight were measured, there was no means of calculating how increased insight improved the client's life situation. Equally, no measurement in Phase I demonstrated whether non-directive therapy was any more effective than any other type.

FURTHER ANALYSIS:
The "Q Technique"

When Carl Rogers put together a group of graduate students and other professionals at the University of Chicago in 1940, he was beginning a study of psychotherapy that he had been advocating for over a decade. As the initial two studies unfolded, he and the other researchers became acutely aware that there was no tool in existence that measured whether clients believed that they had become better. For Rogers, this measure was by far the most important measurement of all, but no psychological test then used captured this information. William Stephenson, an English researcher then working at the University of Chicago, had developed a system of cards called "Q cards" that Rogers and his group used. Rogers calls the information on these Q cards "a population of self-referent items." They contained statements that were originally extracted from client interviews—self-descriptions gleaned from them during their psychotherapeutic interviews.

Examples of the type of statements to be found on these cards are:

- I am a submissive person.
- I'm afraid of a full-fledged disagreement with a person.
- I am a hard worker.
- I am really disturbed.
- I am likable.

Each client involved in the Phase III study would be given 100 of these Q cards and asked to sort them, usually into nine separate categories. The research subjects sorted the cards according to how similar to themselves the statements were. That is, the first stack would hold cards with descriptions that they felt were the most like themselves, the next stack a little less so, and on until by the ninth pile, the person would feel that most of the expressions on the Q cards did not actually apply to them. As only a set number of cards could be sorted into any one pack, the responses were set up to provide a bell-shaped curve which made for more manageable development of statistics. These "Q Sorts" as they were called were done several times during therapy, and in three different ways. The test that Rogers and the others developed from this method came to be called the "SIO (self, ideal, and ordinary) Q Sort" test.

The three methods of sorting the Q cards performed by the study subjects (and the controls) were:

- Categorizing the self-referent statements as to which were the most descriptive of them to those that were least like themselves. This first sort would establish a self-concept.

- Dividing the cards based upon the subject's perception of which cards described best what they would want to be like. This process would extend to a ninth stack that contained statements expressing what the person would least want to be like. This second sort would provide the person's perception of their ideal self.

- Sorting the cards based on the clients' perceptions of "ordinary people." This third sort represented the ordinary data point.

This self-test, given at key points both before, during, and after a client underwent psychotherapy for the first time produced a means of measuring whether or not a person's self-concept actually changed as a result of psychotherapy. The control subjects provided the means of assuring that changes in the people studied were not simply random phenomena, or changes that could have happened anyway, with or without therapy. The Rogers group researchers produced results that were among the most definitive and dramatic ever demonstrated. They showed through their testing methods that people involved in client-centered therapy reduced the gap between their self-concept and their idealized version of themselves. Self-concepts in particular showed drastic improvement.

The second phase of research looked at the efficacy of Rogerian psychotherapy by using more sophisticated, time-tested psychological evaluation. The problem with Phase II, even with the use of improved testing, was twofold: the number of clients involved in the study was small; and there were no experimental "control" subjects involved. Yet, it represented an improvement over the earlier phase of testing.

Among the psychological tests used in Phase II were:

- The Rorschach, or "inkblot" projective test, designed to reveal the subject's inner personality structure, including introversive and extroversive tendencies.

- The MMPI (Minnesota Multiphase Personality Inventory), a questionnaire designed to sort the person's response into certain diagnostic categories in order to indicate his or her tendency toward that diagnosis.

- A client self-rating of improvement scale developed by the researchers.

Ever persuasive, Rogers managed to obtain several hundreds of thousands of dollars in funding from various foundations and from the U.S. Public Health Service to carry out Phase III. Though 15 to 30 people worked on various phases of this research over the years, only 10 of them, including Rogers, remained involved from the project's earliest days until the completion of the third phase. The others were graduate students that became involved for a time and eventually moved on. As noted previously, rather than conduct the research himself, Rogers preferred to facilitate, providing funding, ideas, and simple encouragement. Most of his graduate students came from what was known as "The Rogers Group" at the University of Chicago Counseling Center.

Phase III, the final and most definitive phase of Rogers's research into the efficacy of psychotherapy, was characterized by several innovative ideas, organized as follows:

- The study was divided into two "blocks" of clients, people who had come to the counseling center for help and had agreed to be involved in several batteries of psychological tests during their treatment.
- Block I contained 25 clients who had come for therapy.
- Block II, assembled later, contained at least 25 more clients.
- The ethical problem concerning finding "controls," people not receiving therapy to measure against those receiving therapy, was resolved in two ways: volunteers not receiving therapy but taking the psychological tests used were "matched" to clients in therapy; and prospective clients were put on a waiting list for therapy, and also received the same psychological testing.
- The measurement that Rogers considered

the most important—the client's self-rating of the efficacy of therapy—still needed to be developed. All previous such self-rating scales had proven inaccurate and unscientific. A British researcher, William Stephenson developed the "Q Technique" that finally solved this quandary. (See sidebar)

With the Q Technique in place, Rogers's researchers were ready. "Test Points," times that tests would be administered, were established at key times both before, during, and after therapy. The same battery of tests was administered to the control subjects on much the same schedule: before their wait began, during the clients' psychotherapy treatment, and afterward. The thoroughness of the testing and follow-up clearly demonstrate the painstaking accuracy that was involved in completing this research (as shown below). The detail involved is both impressive and shows clearly why Rogers's research was so heralded by nearly everyone in the mental health field.

Testing and other data collected during Phase III of Rogers' research included:

- A short personal history form filled out by both clients and controls prior to the beginning of treatment.
- A psychological test known as the Willoughby Emotional Maturity Test completed by two of the subject's friends or

relatives, assessing the person's emotional maturity during therapy.

- Recording and transcription of all therapy sessions.

- A SIO (self, ideal, and ordinary) sorting of Q cards prior to therapy, after counseling was completed, and then again six months later. (This was in addition to Q sorts at the seventh, twentieth and, if necessary, at the fortieth counseling session.)

- The Willoughby Emotional Maturity Test to the client administered before, after, and six months after completion of therapy.

- The Thematic Apperception Test (known as the TAT), a projective psychological test similar to the Rorschach, given before, after, and six months after completion of therapy.

- The Self-Other Attitude Scale, a test that measured several social and political attitudes of the person, given on that same schedule of before, after, and six months after completion of psychotherapy sessions.

- A role-playing activity, developed to determine how the client would respond to those around him or her in certain situations.

- In order to assess the therapist's empathy, at the end of the therapy the person conducting the therapy was asked to sort the Q cards as he or she believed the client would.

- A self-rating scale for the therapist appraising their view of the relationship between therapist and client, as well as the entire therapeutic process.

- Two follow-up interviews: one between the client and therapist and one with the client and the person performing the tests to determine the client's assessment of the efficacy of the therapy.

- A follow-up questionnaire sent to clients after the termination of therapy.

CHRONOLOGY

1902: Carl Rogers is born in Oak Park, Illinois.

1914: Moves to a rural Illinois community with his family.

1921: Travels to the Far East with a religious student group.

1924: Graduates from the University of

Wisconsin and marries Helen Elliot.

1926: Son David is born. Leaves seminary to attend Columbia University.

1931: Earns a PhD in psychotherapy from Columbia University.

1940: Receives a full professorship at Ohio State University.

1945: Joins faculty at the University of Chicago. Elected president of the American Psychological Association.

1964: Elected "Humanist of the Year" by the American Humanist Association.

1970: *On Encounter Groups* published. He would publish two more books before his death.

1986: Travels to Russia to facilitate conflict resolution.

1987: Dies of heart attack.

This research, the culmination of years of work and the collaboration of many was, as Rogers freely admitted in his 1954 book *Psychotherapy and Personality Change,* "far from perfect." However, no one had ever before come close to actually measuring what occurred in psychotherapy. The Distinguished Scientific Contribution award given by the American Psychological Association to Rogers in 1956 cited him

for developing an original method to

objectify the description and analysis of the therapeutic process, for formulating a testable theory of psychotherapy and its effects on personality and behavior.... His imagination, persistence and flexible adaptation of scientific method in his attack on the formidable problems involved in the understanding and modification of the individual person has moved this area of psychological interest within the boundaries of scientific psychology.

Rogers cried when he received this honor and even years later said, "Never have I been so emotionally affected . . ."

Case studies

This description of the group process as perceived by Rogers, then 75 years of age, is taken from his 1977 book *Carl Rogers on Personal Power.* It concerns a group held during a workshop Rogers was attending. He describes two of the people in the group, and with tremendous self-honesty, explains how he feels about the interactions occurring between him and these two people. Ben is an elderly psychiatrist attending the group who seems to want Rogers to be an authority and impart wisdom about therapy. Ben also wishes to tell the group his own philosophy—that feelings create nothing but problems and he has been able to live successfully for several years holding all of his emotions in check. Rogers sees the attempt to make him an authority by Ben as "dependency" and admits that it annoys him. Others in the group, especially the women, are angered by Ben's credo regarding feelings and attack him on this score. Rogers feels very impatient, keeps thinking that the group is moving very slowly, and they should pick up the pace.

BIOGRAPHY:
Hazel Markus

"It struck me as an interesting possibility."

That was how, in an interview, Hazel Rose Markus described her initial decision to make social psychology her life work. It is clear Markus' work and ideas had their early development in the theories of Carl Rogers. Like Rogers, Markus began her career in the Midwest, at the University of Michigan. She had received her B.A. from California State University in San Diego, and in 1975 she earned her Ph.D. from the University of Michigan. Unlike Rogers, Helen Markus married a fellow academic; University of Michigan professor Robert Zajonc. She joined the faculty of Stanford University as a professor of psychology in 1994. Markus's career has also included a stint as a research scientist at the Institute of Social Research. Also, like Rogers, Markus has traveled worldwide in the course of her work, has written extensively, and much of her career has been spent studying the self—specifically, self-concept and self-esteem, and how these relate to a person's behavior and his or her interactions with the world.

Markus' other field of endeavor has been one that humanist (and social) psychologists such as Rogers, Karen Horney, and Erich Fromm could surely relate to: the study of how environment and culture relate to the development of the personality. Her research has taken her to places as diverse as Japan and Jamaica. As she describes it, "Specifically, my work is concerned with how gender, ethnicity, religion, social class, cohort, or region or country of natural origin may influence thought and feeling . . . particularly self-relevant thought and feeling." A recent study by Markus addressed the differences in both functioning and self-concept between Japanese and American university students. In combination with Kitayama, Heiman, and Mullally, Markus has written several books and articles, including "A Collective Fear of the Collective: Implications for Selves and Theories for Selves," published in 1994 in the *Personality and Social Psychology Bulletin, Culture and Basic Psychological Principles,* and *Social Psychology: Handbook of Basic Principles.* Markus has also worked on research into shyness, midlife, and aging. Her most current writing, also in conjunction with S. Kitayama, is a book called *Collective Self-Schemas: The Socio-Cultural Grounding of the Personal.*

Michelle, a pretty 30-something divorced woman, expresses both her desire for, and fear of, getting into another relationship. She spoke of going to a swimming pool with a male acquaintance and feeling panic, which caused her to just leave without any explanation. She refers to her ambivalence regarding getting into another relationship by saying, "I'm always doing this push-pull thing. It's awful. I can't bear this stress." Ben then spoke up again, stating that he had been thinking about his no-emotions stance, and realizing that perhaps he was wrong. He goes on to remember that his wife bitterly complained about his being cold and unfeeling, and he now wonders if he is not doing the same thing with this group. Rogers is skeptical of this sudden transformation in Ben. He is also feeling a strong urge to hug Michelle. He tries to question his own reasons for this, and he considers that it is possibly a sexual attraction for her that he is feeling. He finally asks her if she would like a hug, and she replies, "I'd love it!" Rogers hugs her and she says, "Maybe I won't fly home tomorrow after all." (She apparently was having so much difficulty interacting with others that she had considered just leaving the group.)

Based upon the group interactions that Rogers experienced while attending this group, he was able to make the following conclusions about the group process:

- There is power built into a group. The group proceeds at its own pace, and it will not be manipulated or pressured to go either faster or more slowly.

- Risk-taking leads to trust between people in the group. Rogers took responsibility for honestly sharing how he felt and was accepted by the group.

- The psychiatrist Ben also took the risk of sharing, and even though the group was critical of his stance regarding feelings, they were also able to demonstrate to him that they cared.

- Michelle, too, shared her pain and confusion regarding her feelings with the group and felt accepted and cared for by the group.

- Rogers's intuitive action of hugging Michelle proved to be an example for him that his intuition was indeed trustworthy and the group's reaction could also be trusted.

- In the group, closeness was found to be safe.

- The group comes to understand that it is accountable for itself; each member is responsible for expressing themselves to make the group useful to all.

BIBLIOGRAPHY

Sources

Boeree, C. George. *Personality Theories/Carl Rogers.* 2000. http://www.ship.edu/~cgboeree/fromm.html.

Coleman, James. *Abnormal Psychology and Modern Life.* Chicago: Scott, Foresman and Co.,1956.

Goodwin, C.J. *A History of Modern Psychology.* New York: John Wiley and Sons, 1999.

Hazel Markus, Professor of Psychology. 2001. http://www.stanford.edu.

Humanistic Psychologists. *Carl Rogers: His Life and Background.* 2000. http://www.facultyweb.cortland.edu.

Kaplan, Harold I., MD, and Benjamin J. Sadock, MD. *Synopsis of Psychiatry, Behavioral Sciences and Clinical Psychiatry.* Baltimore, MD: William and Wilkins, 1991.

Kirschenbaum, Howard. *On Becoming Carl Rogers.* New York: Delacorte Press, 1979.

Kirschenbaum, Howard and Valerie Henderson. *The Carl Rogers Reader.* Houghton Mifflin, 1989.

Notes on Carl Rogers. 2002. http://www.sonoma.edu.

O'Hara, Maureen. *About Carl Rogers*. 2002. http://www.saybrook.edu.

Rogers, Carl. *Carl Rogers on Encounter Groups*. New York: Harper and Row, 1970.

Rogers, Carl. *Carl Rogers on Personal Power*. New York: Dell Publishing, 1977.

Rogers, Carl. *Client-Centered Therapy: Its Current Practice, Implications and Theory*. Boston: Houghton Mifflin, 1951.

Rogers, Carl. *Counseling and Psychotherapy: Newer Concepts in Practice*. Boston: Houghton Mifflin, 1942.

Rogers, Carl. *On Becoming a Person*. Boston: Houghton Mifflin, 1961.

Rogers, Carl. *Psychotherapy and Personality Change*. Chicago: University of Chicago Press, 1954.

Rogers, Carl. *A Way of Being*. New York: Houghton Mifflin, 1980.

Further readings

Rogers, Carl. *The Clinical Treatment of the Problem Child*. Boston: Houghton Mifflin, 1939.

Rogers, Carl. *Counseling with Returned Servicemen*. New York: McGraw-Hill, 1946.

Rogers, Carl. *A Therapist's View of Personal Goals*. Wallingford, PA: Pendle Hill, 1965.

Rogers, Carl. *The Therapeutic Relationship and its*

Impact. Madison, WI: University of Wisconsin Press, 1967.

Rogers, Carl. *Person to Person: The Problem of Being Human, A New Trend in Psychology.* Lafayette, CA: Real People Press, 1967.

Rogers, Carl. *Freedom to Learn: A View of What Education Might Become.* Columbus, OH: Macmillan, 1969.

Rogers, Carl. *Freedom to Learn: Studies of the Person.* Columbus, OH: Charles E. Merrill, 1969.

Rogers, Carl. *Becoming Partners: Marriage and its Alternatives.* New York: Delacorte Press, 1972.

Rogers, Carl. *Freedom to Learn for the Eighties.* New York: Prentice Hall, 1983.

Lightning Source UK Ltd.
Milton Keynes UK
UKHW021103261020
372252UK00016B/1266